NATIONAL GEOGRAPHIC

Frogs

Norman Yu

This is a spotted grass frog.
Like all frogs, it is an amphibian.
This means it lives in the water
when it is born.
When it is older, it can live
on land, too.

The spotted grass frog begins its life as a tiny egg.
Many eggs float in the water.
The outside of each egg is clear.
Inside each egg is a tiny tadpole.

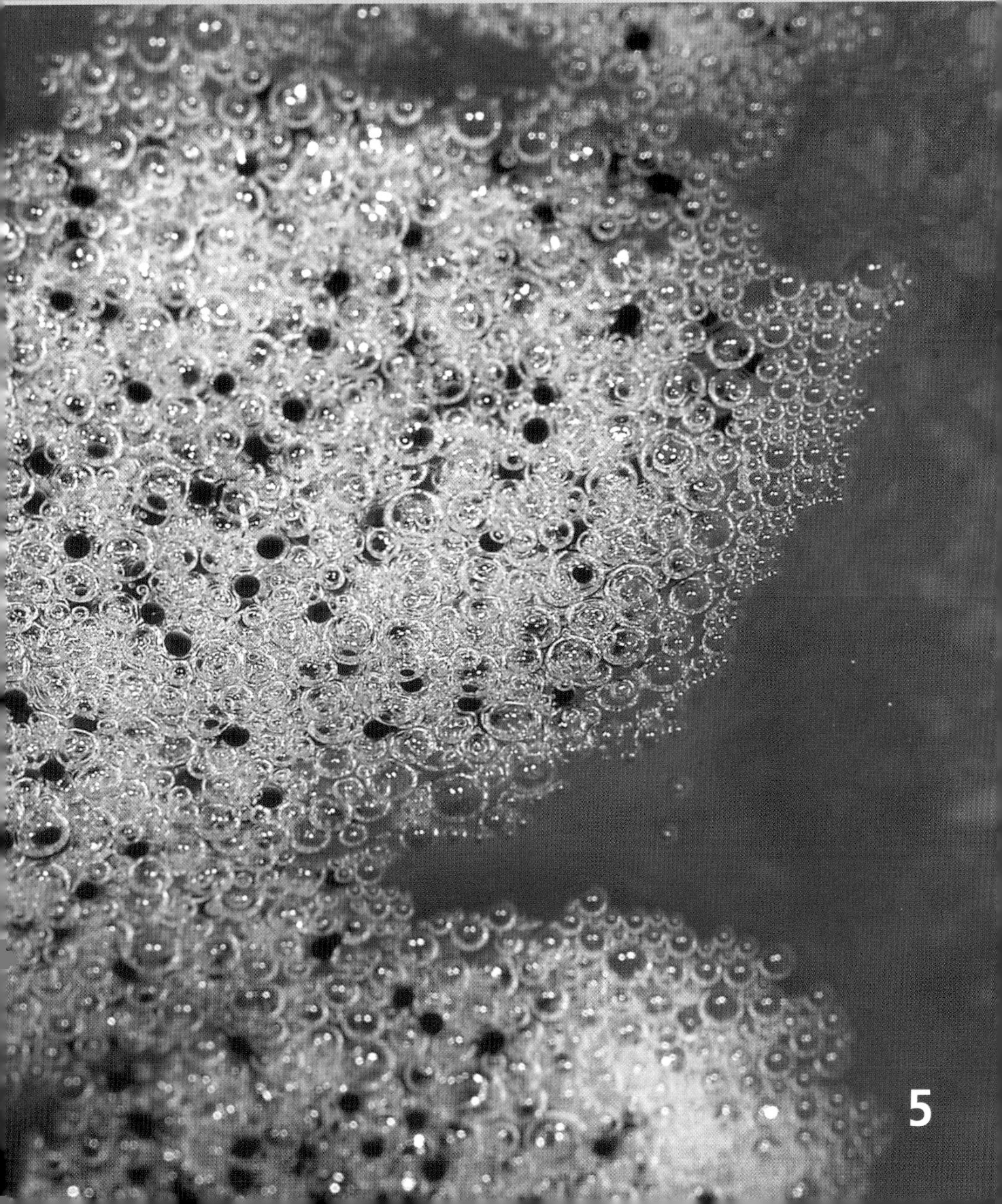

The tadpoles hatch from the eggs. Tadpoles have small, round bodies and long tails.

The tadpoles live in the water.
They have gills so they can
breathe underwater.
They have a long tail to help
them swim.

As the tadpole grows bigger,
it begins to change.
The tadpole grows back legs.
It grows front legs, too.
The tadpole also grows lungs.
Its lungs will let it breathe on land.

Finally, the tadpole's tail disappears.
Now it is a frog.
The frog has legs for jumping
and lungs for breathing.
It is ready to live on the land.

The spotted grass frog goes through many changes.

tadpole

tadpole
with legs

Glossary

amphibians animals that live in the water and on land

gills the parts of the body that let some animals breathe underwater

hatch when a young animal comes out of an egg

lungs the parts of the body used to breathe air

tadpole a young animal that will become a frog as it gets older